Visit me for more great insights on
www.andrewstotz.com

Also by Dr. Andrew Stotz
Transform Your Business with Dr. Deming's 14 Points

Dr. Andrew Stotz

How to Start Building Your Wealth Investing in the Stock Market

A Note to the Reader

This book is written and designed to provide accurate and authoritative information on the subject of personal finances. The contents of this book are intended as a general guide on the personal finance topics covered in it. If professional advice is needed, you should seek advice from qualified legal and/or financial professionals about your individual financial plan and situation. The book is sold with the understanding that neither the Author nor the Publisher is engaged in rendering legal, accounting or other professional services by publishing this book.

As of the date of publishing, all contents in the book, such as information, data, and web links are accurate and up to date to the best knowledge of the Author and Publisher. The Author and Publisher cannot be held responsible for any inaccuracies.

The Author and the Publisher specifically deny responsibility for any liability, loss or risk that may be suffered as a consequence of, indirectly or directly, applying any of the ideas contained in this book.

ISBN: 1536968538
ISBN-13: 978-1-5369685-3-8

DEDICATION

Thanks to my Mom and Dad, who never gave up on me.

CONTENTS

ACKNOWLEDGMENTS

Thanks to all those who have helped me grow and learn throughout my whole life. Nikki Babbit and Mike Matoney deserve special mention for helping me learn to open my mind and my heart. A big thanks to my long time business partner and great friend, Sornsak Kongcharoenpanich, for all the fantastic years of finance research and discovery. Thanks must also go to all five of my nieces: Kristin Wyke, Audrey Wyke, Sophie Wyke, Hannah Eastman and especially Elsie Eastman, who worked tirelessly with me to better craft this book's message. Thanks to Alexander Wetterling for helping me move from my original idea to this book. A special thanks to my chief editor, Bevan Powrie, who went through every word, over and over, helping me to sharpen my expression.

INTRODUCTION:
WHERE DID THIS BOOK COME FROM?

In this book, I will teach you 12 investment principles that will help you manage your money for the rest of your life. If you have little or no experience with investing, this book is for you! My hope is that once you have read it, you will take charge of your financial future and start making smart financial decisions on your own.

What inspired me to create this course?

My five nieces once asked me, "Uncle Andrew, how can we take care of our money? Can you teach us about investing? Do you think we could get rich in the stock market?"

I honed this course by teaching each of my nieces how to invest their money and secure their financial futures. I wanted to help them become financially independent, and now that I have taught them, I want to teach you.

You may not be as interested in finance as I am. My nieces were not. They, like most beginners, needed clear and simple guidance that they could understand and follow. In this book, we will go through this guidance, step by step, so that you can learn how to secure your financial future, just as my nieces have.

A word about the word "rich" – the sad truth is that no matter how much we dream about it, most of us will never be rich in the traditional sense (as in, being a multimillionaire). However, I do not believe that being rich is the main objective in life, and I know it is not the goal of many people. To me, being rich means knowing that I can take care of myself and my family financially; that I have made financial plans for my future and that I am investing accordingly. It means that I do not have to worry about my financial situation, because I know that I will have enough money.

For most, the road to riches is a six-stage process. First, getting out of debt. Second, saving some money. Third, starting to invest. Fourth, starting to receive dividends on those investments. Fifth, building up the size of investments. And sixth, receiving enough investment income to pay for monthly living costs.

It is my hope that I can successfully guide you through these six stages, as I have with my nieces. If I accomplish this, I will have achieved what I set out to do with this book.

What is NOT in this book?
I have been asked many times during my travels while giving the companion seminar to this book why I did not include topics such as inflation and dollar-cost averaging. The answer is, to make this book as simple as possible for beginners, I excluded everything that I considered not crucial to explaining the 12 basic elements to help young people with managing money over a lifetime. For those seeking to go into the subject in more detail, you are welcome to join the discussion at www.andrewstotz.com/blog. See you there!

1. CREATE A WRITTEN PLAN AND FOLLOW IT

What are the advantages of having a written plan?

1.   Writing your plan down forces you to make decisions that you might never have thought about when your plan was just in your head. Your "mental plan" is probably far less complete than you think.

2.   A written plan helps you conquer the tricks that your mind and the stock market play on you. Once you commit your mental plan to paper, you will have a solid road map to follow in times of doubt, stress, and volatility, which are the major contributors to the state of mind that causes the most financial damage: panic.

3.   Referencing a written plan helps you to visualize your financial goals and remind yourself of what you want. It keeps you focused on how much to save in order to achieve financial security.

4.   A written plan helps you overcome "overconfidence bias", the feeling that not only can you do it, not only can you handle it, but that you are better than average. Many research papers[1] have shown that all of us have the behavioral bias of overconfidence. Sometimes, you may feel less confident (like when you're going into an exam you did not study for), but in

general, we all face overconfidence bias in our lives.

One other benefit of having a good financial plan and executing it over time is that it helps you to ensure that you will not be a burden on your children later in life. This will give them the freedom to make their own financial choices without having to worry about you. I am happy that my mother and father had a strong financial plan. As a consequence, they are not a burden on my sister and me. I challenge you to become independent and not be a burden on others when you get older. Start with a written plan.

This may surprise you, but most people do not have a written financial plan[2] even though making one is one of the most beneficial things you can do to ensure future financial success. Today, you are going to make your written plan and begin taking responsibility for your financial future.

Consider how we view planning in other areas of life. I am currently considering building a house and have been meeting with an architect. She asks me so many questions!

Architect: "How big do you want the house?"

Andrew: "Well … medium sized."

Architect: "No, I need exact numbers."

Andrew: "Okay."

Architect: "How many rooms do you want?"

Andrew: "Well, how about three?"

Architect: "Okay, three's fine. How big do you want them?"

Andrew: "Well, I want them big."

Architect: "How big?"

Andrew: "Well, big, like other rooms!"

Architect: "No, I need exact measurements – I need to know in square feet, even square inches!"

Any architect knows that you cannot just start building without a written plan. You need to have the blueprint and the instructions set before you can build anything. I want you to be like an architect, with a written plan when you start, so you do not get lost along the way.

What about overestimation bias? We overestimate things all

the time – how well we will perform on an exam, how much control we have in our lives, and the speed with which we can get work done[3]. Academic studies have shown[4] that experts are the worst offenders! Because of their expert status, their confidence level is high. But research has shown[5] that often their actual results are not as good as they expect them to be. Regardless, you do not have to be an expert to create a great financial plan. Your plan should be simple enough for you to follow, and should include these six parts:

1. Your investment and retirement horizon
2. How much money you will need
3. How much to contribute on a regular basis
4. What risk and return to expect
5. Your asset allocation
6. Monitoring and rebalancing plan

These steps are not complex, but there is a lot to think about that you may never have considered. Once you get these six steps written out, you will have a fantastic plan that you can understand and follow.

Let's start with this question: have you thought about when you will retire? If you are young, you might never have thought about it; I certainly didn't think about retirement when I was young. But answering this question today is the first concrete step toward making realistic financial goals for your lifetime.

You also need to think about how long you are going to live. If you're going to live to be 100, that's a long time to support yourself in retirement.

To get started, here are some questions for you to complete. "I am _____ years old and I want to retire when I am _____. I will live a happy life until I am _____." Start your plan by writing down your answers. Of course, nobody knows when they will die, but it is better to make a plan with a specific age in mind than to allow your uncertainty to prevent you from making a plan at all.

Great! Now you are on your way to creating a great

financial plan. Chapter one detailed how to create a written plan and follow it. Now that you have begun making a plan, let's move to Chapter two. Are you ready?

Change the way you think about it:

- Creating a written plan is probably the best way to ensure your financial success. Most people do not have one, but now you are not most people.
- Your written plan should cover these six things: your investment and retirement horizon, how much money you will need, how much to contribute on a regular basis, what risk and return to expect, your asset allocation, and monitoring and rebalancing.

New terms:

- **Allocation** – The amount you have in various types of assets. For example, when you are in your 20s, the portion of your investment money allocated to stocks should be about 90%. The rest should be allocated to bonds.
- **Rebalance** – To buy or sell a portion of assets that you own to make sure that they remain in the proportion you want for the best result over time.
- **Return** – When you put $100 in the bank and at the end of the year, you earn $3 in interest, the $3 is your return. To calculate your return, divide your earnings ($3) by your original investment ($100). In this case, your return was 3%. With stocks, a return has two parts: a dividend (like this 3% example) and a capital gain (or the increase in the stock's price). So, if you bought a stock at the beginning of the year for $100, you received $3 in dividends, and you sold the stock for $104 at the end of the period, your return would be $3 (dividend) plus $4 (capital gain), or $7. This number divided by $100 shows that, in this case, you earned a 7% return.
- **Stock** – A physical or electronic document that shows what amount of a company you own. It's also called a

share. Businesses issue shares to the people who invest money in them. These people are called shareholders.

- **Stock market** – An actual or virtual place to buy or sell shares of a business.
- **Stock market index** – An accumulation of many stock prices into one price that is used to understand whether the overall stock market has gone up or down.
- **Volatility** – The tendency of stock and bond prices to move up and down, often quickly and unpredictably.
- **Financial independence** – To be financially independent means that the investment income you earn from your stock & bond portfolios (which we will discuss in the following chapters) is enough to cover your living expenses. The goal of this book is to help you become financially independent by the time you retire.

2. SIMPLICITY BEATS COMPLEXITY; KEEP IT SIMPLE

If your financial plan is too complicated, you will not follow it! Keeping it simple will help you to stay on track. And remember: having more information does not mean you will make better decisions. It is only *correct* information that will help you make better decisions.

Financial institutions and advisors will often provide you with a lengthy financial plan containing a lot of details. They do this because they want to cover all bases. It may seem powerful and impressive, but is that the best financial plan for you? If it is so complex that you need someone to help you follow it, it will be hard for you to reach financial independence. It is better to start by focusing on a plan that is simple enough for you to follow on your own.

Some studies have shown[6] that when you give people more information before they make a decision, their confidence level rises, but their decision-making does not improve. This is important because the world is full of information, particularly in the financial world. Newspapers, magazines, TV, and online content bombard us every day. Think of it this way: Imagine you want to cross the street. Even that simple task throws a lot of information at you! You see the billboard across the road. Your friend is talking to you. Your phone rings. Another friend is on the other side of the road beckoning to you. The amount of information around you is endless, but what is the only information that matters? What matters in this case is whether or not there is a bus coming toward you, about to run you over! So remember, the only thing you need to process is the information that is most important.

When investing in the stock market, you have three main options: own one stock, own all stocks, or own some number of stocks between these two extremes. In the first case, you expose yourself to "company-specific risk". This is the risk that the company whose shares you own goes bankrupt and their share price collapses, leaving you with nothing.

Share price collapses happen more often than you might think. I have known some people who made the decision to buy one stock at the recommendation of a friend, and then lost almost all their money because that particular stock collapsed. Then they tell me they never want to invest in the stock market again. But, the reality is that by buying only one stock, they took on unnecessary risk. They thought that stock would be a winner, and risked their money on it, but it turned out to be a loser. They may not have known how much risk they were really taking on, but unfortunately for them, the world does not care when people do not know they are taking on excessive company-specific risk.

YOUR SEATBELT: Reduce risk related to owning stocks

Types of Investment risks	What is the risk?	Owning fewer stocks	Owning more stocks
Company-Specific risk	One company's stock price falls	Increases	Decreases
Market risk	The whole market falls	No impact	No impact

Figure 1. Major risks related to stock market investing.

If you owned all stocks in the stock market, company-specific risk would not affect you, because when one stock crashes, another rises. Of course, you would still be exposed to (stock) "market risk" – the risk that the whole stock market could collapse. If that were to happen, you would lose some value in your portfolio, but not all the value, as you would in the case of owning only one stock of a company that went bankrupt. If you owned all stocks, you would miss the big gains that can come from owning one great stock, but the trade-off is that your portfolio would never collapse completely. If you choose to invest your money by building a portfolio of stocks on your own, you should understand these two risks first. So, how can you balance risk and return?

Successful investors usually have their own personal methods for picking stocks. One method might be to buy the stocks of companies that are cheaply priced in the stock market. Another method could be to buy the stocks of high-quality companies. There are many stock-picking methods followed by investors around the world. Once an investor builds a list of stocks that fit their method, they might choose to buy three to five stocks from the top of their list.

On the other hand, if an investor held 100 stocks, their portfolio would be so diversified that it would look and behave nothing like the few stocks chosen by means of their original method. This raises a key question: If you were picking your own stocks, what would be the right number of stocks to own in a portfolio?

My research[7] and my experience show that if you are going to pick stocks on your own and build your own portfolio, you should own no fewer than 10 stocks. Ten is a number small enough to allow you to stay true to your method, giving you a chance to beat the market's return, but it is large enough to protect your portfolio from being damaged if any single stock drops significantly. So, owning 10 stocks reduces the majority of unnecessary company-specific risk.

Deciding which 10 stocks you should own is a little more complex. How can you find the best 10 stocks? How should you track them? How would you know when to sell one of your stocks? You would have to keep a close eye on company-specific news and watch quarterly profit announcements for all your stocks. You would end up doing the job of a fund manager! Is that what you want to do with your time? Some people want to become fund managers because they love picking stocks. But, not everyone wants to do that. For some people, like my nieces, it is much too complicated – even boring! If you do not want to be responsible for picking individual stocks, don't worry. There are other ways to invest, which we will get into later.

Let's get back to this step's primary goal: keeping it simple. If you do plan to pick stocks, the most important thing to know is that owning 10 stocks reduces a large amount of unnecessary company-specific risk, just like wearing a seatbelt reduces unnecessary risk in a car.

Imagine that a Martian visits earth, stands at the side of a road, sees a car approaching, flags down the driver and asks him, "Hey, can I drive your car?" The driver agrees, quickly explains the gas, brakes, and steering wheel, and the Martian speeds away. He drives as fast as the car can go, loses control, and hits a tree. Crash! He flies through the windshield and gets crushed. Why did this happen? Because the Martian did not know what that strap that goes over you and buckles into the seat was. He did not know that there was a seatbelt that could protect him while driving, and he paid the price for his ignorance.

You wear a seatbelt in a car because you understand how it can reduce the risk of injury in case of an accident. But, because this driver was an alien from Mars, he had no idea what it was or why he should wear it.

Did the world care that he did not know what a seatbelt was? Of course not! The world does not care if you take unnecessary risks. To reduce the risk of losing your money in the stock market, you should consider owning 10 stocks to be as essential to your long-term wellbeing as wearing your seatbelt in a car.

In 2008, two professors reviewed a survey of a large number of US investors that had asked how many stocks they held in their portfolios.[8] You now know that a person who picks stocks should own about 10 stocks in their portfolio to reduce most of their company-specific risk. How many stocks do you think the investors had? Take a guess! Keep in mind that over the years there has been a lot of academic research on the subject of how many stocks an individual should hold. For almost 40 years, this information has been free and available to the public! If any of these investors wanted to know how many stocks they should hold, they could access it for free and would know how to reduce their company-specific risk in the market by owning at least 10 stocks. They could all know about the seatbelt! But, as we all know, not everyone wears a seatbelt.

The results of the study showed that 75% of the investors surveyed owned five or fewer stocks. Fifty percent owned only one or two stocks! The important thing to learn from this research is that most people take on much more risk in the stock market than they need to. They do not wear their seatbelts. From today on, you need to be smarter than that, and wear your financial seatbelt!

We started this chapter talking about simplicity, but have ended with complexity – the complexity of picking 10 stocks and managing that portfolio of stocks. You might wonder how you could manage your own portfolio of 10 stocks, or you might think, like my nieces, you do not want to be responsible for picking stocks. We will soon discuss these problems and you will see how you can reduce your company-specific risk in a very simple way, a way that does not require you to pick your own portfolio of 10 stocks.

Change the way you think about it:
- Keep it simple – only pay attention to the information that is most important. Block out the rest.
- Owning stocks exposes you to company-specific and market risk.
- To eliminate unnecessary company-specific risk you

should hold at least 10 stocks. Consider this level of diversification as your seatbelt.

- Most people are probably not suited for or interested in buying individual stocks. For these people, there is a better way of investing, which we will discuss in the following chapters.

New terms:

- **Active investor** – Someone who actively trades stocks to try to time the market and pick the most attractive stocks. Ultimately they want to beat the market.
- **Beat the market** – A term used in the world of finance when we discuss the objective of most investors, especially active investors or stock pickers. To beat the market, or get a higher return than the market, one must choose stocks that are outperforming other stocks in the market.
- **Company-specific risk** – The risk that you buy the stock of one company and that company's stock price collapses. This risk nearly disappears if you hold 10 or more stocks because as one stock goes down, another is likely to go up.
- **Diversification** – Buying more than one stock for your portfolio. The benefit of diversifying your portfolio is that you reduce company-specific risk.
- **Portfolio** – A collection of stocks.
- **Stock market risk** – (Also called market risk) The risk that the stock market falls as a whole. If this happens, nearly every stock in the market will fall, including the stocks in your portfolio. Once you have removed company-specific risk from your portfolio, market risk remains. It is hard to avoid this risk unless you can somehow successfully predict when to get out of (and get back into) the market. This is unlikely.

3. START EARLY; TIME REALLY IS MONEY!

We must get into the right frame of mind when we invest in the stock market. Starting with an "I'm going to get rich quick" attitude will rarely lead to success. The good news is that there is one way that you can almost guarantee your financial success in the stock market, and that is to invest over a long period.

Time is money – and the more time you have, the more money you can make. However, to maximize this benefit, you *must* take advantage of the time you have and *start early*. This is one place where young people have a major advantage. When people over 50 attend my seminars they say that they wish they knew about the time value of money when they were younger. You have the chance to learn this now!

The magic of "compound interest", or "the compounding effect", is the most powerful way to be successful in the stock market. There is only one problem: It takes 30 years.

In Chapter one, you decided when you wanted to retire and how long you expect to live. These inputs will help you identify your investment and retirement horizons. Let's consider an example: Assume you are 20 years old, want to retire when you are 70, and expect to live a happy life until you are 90.

To get started, look at Figure 2 and find your age on the vertical axis where it says "Current Age" (for this example, it would be 20). Now look across the table and find the number that represents how old you will be when you finally become financially independent (in this example, the age would be 70). If you look down the column to where the row and column intersect, you will see the number 50. This is your investment horizon, the number of years between today and the year you would like to be financially independent. Use this chart to find your own investment horizon, and write it into the financial plan that you started in Chapter one. If you don't want to use the chart, you can simply take your desired retirement age (70) and subtract your current age (20) to get your investment horizon (50 years).

		Age of Financial Independence					
		40	50	60	70	80	90
Current Age	20	20	30	40	50	60	70
	30	10	20	30	40	50	60
	40	–	10	20	30	40	50
	50	–	–	10	20	30	40
	60	–	–	–	10	20	30
	70	–	–	–	–	10	20
	80	–	–	–	–	–	10
	90	–	–	–	–	–	–
	100	–	–	–	–	–	–

Figure 2. Determine your "investment horizon".

Now let's find your retirement horizon. This is the number of years between the day you become financially independent and the end of your life. If you plan to be financially independent at age 70 and live a happy life until you are 90, you can see from the intersection in Figure 3 that you would have a retirement horizon of 20 years. People often underestimate this period, which is dangerous. This is the period in your life when you will no longer be generating

15

income from work. If you do not plan wisely now, this time could be quite stressful. On the other hand, if you plan ahead, you could spend retirement traveling and enjoying life with your family. If you do not wish to use the chart, you can simply subtract your retirement age from the age you suppose you will live to.

Live Life until this Age	Age of Financial Independence: 40	50	60	70	80	90
20	-	-	-	-	-	-
30	-	-	-	-	-	-
40	-	-	-	-	-	-
50	10	-	-	-	-	-
60	20	10	-	-	-	-
70	30	20	10	-	-	-
80	40	30	20	10	-	-
90	50	40	30	20	10	-
100	60	50	40	30	20	10

Figure 3. Determine your "retirement horizon".

If your investment horizon is 50 years and your retirement horizon is 20 years, you will be managing your money for 70 years! That is a long time! No one is going to be able to help you throughout that whole period, so you must do it yourself. You feed and clothe yourself for your whole life, right? Well, you can be responsible for your own money as well.

As you begin to think about investing from a longer term perspective, you will understand how silly it sounds when you hear people talk about making short-term gains in the stock market. Now you know – the secret to investing successfully is not about making gains in one week, one month, or even one year. It is about 70 years! Short-term thinking is a mistake.

So, why is starting early the most surefire method for investing in the stock market? Because money in the stock market grows exponentially over time, which is especially evident in later years. However, this only works if you reinvest the dividends and cash flows that you receive from your investments. If you spend, rather than reinvest, your dividends as soon as they appear, you will not benefit from the magic of compounding over time. Compounding interest on interest is CRITICAL to wealth creation! Let's look at this in more detail.

Imagine that you put $100 in the bank and let it sit there for 10 years. Suppose you get a 10% annual interest rate from the bank (highly unrealistic, but easy to understand). After the first year, you will have earned $10 in interest, which you are able to take out and spend, so you buy yourself dinner with it. Then, the next year, you earn another $10 on the $100, and spend that too. By the end of the 10 years, you will have received (and then spent) $100 in interest ($10 each year). That is the same amount that you originally put in! Not bad – you doubled your money. But that is hardly magical.

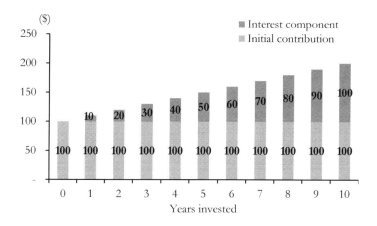

Figure 4. A $100 bank deposit paying a 10% interest rate, assuming you spent the interest component received each year.

The magic of compounding happens when you do not take

out the interest, but rather leave it in the bank to compound on itself. So, let's go back to the end of the first year and say you earned $10, but this time, you leave it in the bank instead of buying yourself dinner. Then, the next year, you receive another 10 dollars on the original $100, but you also earn 10% on the $10 interest you received at the end of the first year. This is where the magic starts! Now you have $121 ($100 original investment, $10 interest from the first year, $1 interest on the $10 from the first year, and then another $10 in interest from the second year). We call that $1 "interest on interest" because you earned it from the interest you earned, not the money you put in. This is the compounding effect. It may look small in the beginning, but trust me, it will grow exponentially, leaving you with much more later on.

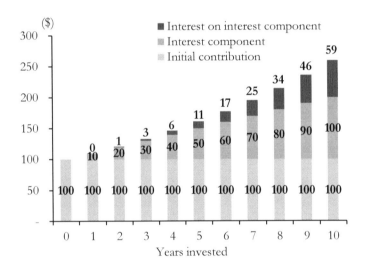

Figure 5. Now the magic starts with interest on interest.

To review, your initial $100 investment will not grow since you did not put more money into the bank, so that portion of the graph stays flat. Your annual interest will accumulate, but in a linear fashion ($10+$10+$10 and so on). It is only the interest on that annual interest that accumulates in an exponential way.

Figures 4 and 5 show only until year 10, so the exponential growth may not seem like much. But imagine that you left the $100 in the bank for 30 years – what would it become?

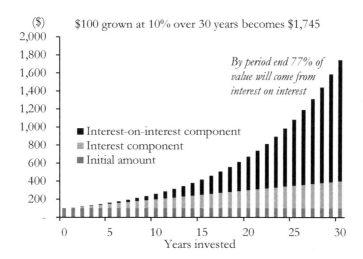

Figure 6. After 30 years, interest on interest dominates.

In Figure 6, note that the interest-on-interest component grows to become almost 80% of the total wealth at the end of the period. This shows that the magic of compounding does not happen in the short term. It only happens over time. So, the surefire method for investing success in the stock market is to start early, because time really is money.

Change the way you think about it:

- Your investment and retirement horizons combined could be longer than 50 years, so stay focused on the long term.
- Compound interest, or "interest on interest" is the only surefire way to grow your wealth in the stock market.
- To get this benefit you must reinvest your interest and

dividends and keep your money in the market for at least 30 years.

New terms:

- **Compound interest** – When you reinvest the interest or dividends you earn on your investments, you receive income on that reinvested money. This is compound interest. Compound interest allows your money to grow exponentially, especially in later years.
- **Dividend** – When a company makes a profit, it can either reinvest it in its business or pay it out as cash to shareholders. This cash paid to shareholders is called a dividend. It is similar to interest you receive from a bank, but the main difference is that the company has the choice to pay it or not, which makes it riskier than interest earned from a bank.
- **Investment horizon** – The number of years between today and the year you would like to be financially independent. During this time, you are generating income from work and it is your time to save and invest aggressively. You should stay invested and reinvest all earnings.
- **Retirement horizon** – The number of years between the day you become financially independent and the end of your life. During this time you will no longer generate income from work; therefore you must protect your wealth carefully. You will no longer contribute money to your investments, rather you will start to live off of this wealth.

4. BE REALISTIC ABOUT STOCK MARKET RETURNS

I have a message for you to remember for the rest of your life, but you may not like it. Are you ready?

You won't get rich in the stock market.

To be successful in the stock market, I recommend you approach investing with this philosophy.

Imagine you were going to a casino for the first time. You say to your friends, "I am going to get rich in that casino." You are so confident that you go to your family and friends and say "Give me all the money you have – I'm going to the casino and I am going to get rich!" Is that the right mentality to have? Of course not! You could lose all your money in the blink of an eye! To be successful in the stock market, you must approach it with appropriate expectations, just as you should a casino.

Recently, I was looking at the Forbes 400 list of the richest people in the world, and I noticed that 79 of them were listed under these categories: hedge funds, investments, money management, and private equity. But, when I looked deeper into this list I found that, though many of them were successful in the stock market, their real riches came from starting fund-management businesses. In other words, almost none of the people on that Forbes 400 list are rich because they are stock traders – rather, they got rich because they were very successful businesspeople!

So, here is what I have learned from 20 years of experience in the stock market with some of the world's top financial experts: If you really want to get rich, become an entrepreneur. Start a successful business. If it's not in your blood to become an entrepreneur, find an entrepreneur and help them build a successful business. Building businesses to create products and services that the world needs is how most people get rich.

You might ask, "What about billionaire Warren Buffett? He's at the top of that Forbes list! Isn't he an investor?" Yes, he invests, but Buffett is really a business owner. If you listen to him talk about his style and methods, you will hear him say that he would prefer never to sell his stocks. But, most people do not go into the stock market with that mindset. They want to trade stocks and "play the market". You might ask about George Soros, or other people like him who are also on the Forbes list. I would say, "Yes, there are a few people who have made a huge amount of money from trading in the stock market, just like there are a few people who walk out of the casino with a lot of money. But that's not the outcome you should expect!"

So, I contend that in most cases, the investors on the Forbes list did not get truly rich in the stock market. They may have gotten their start that way, but they truly got rich by starting a stock market hedge fund, or a fund-management business. These are some of the most profitable businesses in the world, and that is where they made a large portion of their money!

Now that you understand what I mean when I say you won't get rich in the stock market, I am going to add the second part of the concept.

Here it is:

You won't get rich in the stock market…

Until you change the way you think about it.

My objective in this book is to get you to change the ways you may have been thinking about the stock market.

To be successful in the stock market, you need to have realistic expectations about long-term stock market returns. Unfortunately, the information we receive is often misleading. You might be talking to friends and, because people love to talk about their stock market winners, someone might say, "I bought that stock at $10, and it went to $100!" or you could be watching TV and hear someone else say, "I bought stock ABC at $100 and it went to $1,000!" Listening to this, it may seem like everyone is making lots of money in the stock market! Unfortunately, you are only hearing half of the story because most people do not tell you about their losers. What really matters is the sum of winners and losers over a long period of time. Remember, your investment and retirement horizons are long. You need to make smart decisions, one after another, throughout the entire period.

What long-term return should you expect from the stock market? If a bank pays 1% interest on your deposit, then the stock market, which exposes you to higher risk, should give you a higher return. Unfortunately, what I have found over the years is that most people's expectations of stock market returns are much too high. What should you expect? Over the last 50 years, the US stock market has risen an average of 10% per year. Of course there were some years which yielded much higher returns and some that yielded much lower. If we extend this discussion to all the stock markets in the world, overall historical results have been about the same on an annual basis.

Since you need to look at your money management timeline in terms of decades, I recommend that you set your expectation of stock market returns to about 8% to be conservative. If your expectations are low and the market return goes to 10%, it will be a happy surprise. But if you set your expectations at 10% and the market produces only 8%, it could be a painful disappointment that could prevent you from hitting your goal of financial independence.

You might say, "But the stock market in my country is up 20% year to date!" Remember that that is only over the course of one year. You now know that you will be investing over many years. In the long run, the return of the stock market will probably average out to 8% to 10%. To conclude, I recommend you expect an 8% return from the stock market. That is realistic.

The bad news is that it is not easy to get rich in the market if you are earning an average of 8% annually. Of course, you could get lucky one year if the market went up by a lot, but it could just as easily go down the next year. Like a person walking into a casino, you should not base your plan on catching one of those unpredictable lucky years. You must invest in the stock market with realistic expectations from the start.

When you invest in the stock market, you will have the best risk/return trade-off if you own all stocks in the market. Trying to time the market is not a wise long-term strategy. But, does the plan of owning all stocks work equally for everyone, no matter what? Well, no.

Imagine that someone put $100 in a stock market fund, and in the next year the stock market fell 20%, reducing their initial investment to $80. Then the market bounced back by 25% the next year, and the investor was back to their original $100. They would break even. But let's say that someone was lucky enough to start investing the second year, after the stock market had already fallen 20%. Their $100 initial investment would grow 25% in their first year of investing without first having the negative impact of the market's fall. The person who started the year before, on the other hand, experienced both the fall and the rise, so he did not make any money – he only broke even. If we now assume that both earn an 8% total return each year over the next 29 years, the first investor would end up with $863, while the second investor would end up with $1,078.

To think about this further, go back to the end of the year

1900 and imagine that a person invested $100 in the stock market that year and then left it to grow for 30 years. In year 1930, based on actual market returns, the final sum would have been $1,080 – about an 8% average annual return. By repeating this for each year (1901 until 1931, 1902 until 1932, and so on), I was able to calculate the returns over 30 years from each starting year until 1984. From this I calculated an average for each decade. I found a 6.8% average annual return for the decade of the 1900-1909. This means that the average person who invested $100 for 30 years, starting in the decade of 1900-1909, would have earned a return of about 6.8%.

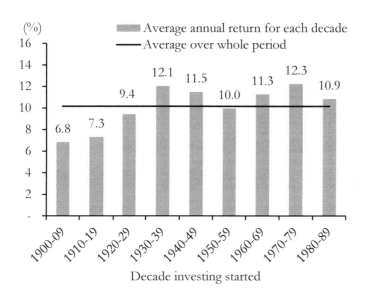

Figure 7. Long term US stock market return of 10%.

In Figure 7, each bar represents the average annual gain of an investor who started to invest in the stock market in that decade, and then left their investment to grow over 30 years. For example, if you started investing in 1910, over the coming 30 years you would have earned an average annual return in the stock market of 7.3%, much lower than if you were lucky enough to have started investing in the 1970s (during that decade, the market was relatively flat and there were no major crashes in the following 30 years, which means that you would be able to start investing at low prices and gain as you go).

Whether the stock market is near long-term highs or lows when you start investing is impossible to know and something you have no control over. Some financial professionals might advise you choose against investing for your first five years and try to wait until the market gets cheap, but then you would miss the compounding effect that you need in order to create wealth. Also, you would need to be able to correctly predict the right time to put your money in, something even the professionals find hard to do.

Now that you know you should expect an 8% return from the stock market, it's time to move on to what you can do to increase your chances of success in the market.

Change the way you think about it:
- Most wealthy people get rich by starting and running successful businesses, not by investing.
- People love to talk about their winners, but what really matters is the sum of your winners and losers over time.
- Over the long term, expect your stock portfolio to earn about 8%.
- When investing for the long term, it doesn't really matter if the market is high or low when you buy stocks.
- If you are unlucky enough to start investing during a decade when the market is expensive, then you may have to contribute more money to achieve your long-term financial goals.
- Even the professionals cannot consistently win at the game of timing when to get into and out of the stock market. Knowing this, you should invest regularly and not worry about timing.

New terms:

- **Capital gain** – When you buy a stock for $100 and sell it for $107, the $7 is your gain, or capital gain. It could also be expressed as 7%.

- **Equity** – When a business owner invests money into her own business, it is called shareholder's equity, or just equity. It is this equity that is bought and sold in the stock market when the company is listed on the stock exchange. Hence, we sometimes call the stock market, the equity market. And we sometimes call stocks "equity".

- **Hedge fund** – A partnership that manages the money of people with high net worth, aggressively trying to beat the market.

- **Time the market** – This refers to the idea that an individual can detect when the stock market is expensive and sell all or a portion of their stocks, and that they can identify when the stock market is cheap and buy back into the market. This would require overcoming the emotional rollercoaster that drives people to sell when the market is down, and vice versa when it is up. It would also require a method of determining if the stock market is expensive or cheap. My experience is that timing the market is extremely difficult for professionals, so what chance would the average investor have?

5. DO IT YOURSELF;
PROS DON'T ALWAYS WORK FOR YOU

If you think you should be picking your own stocks, I have a few questions for you.

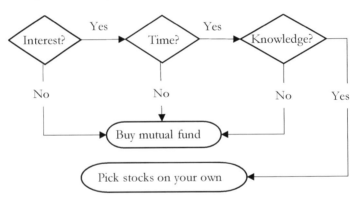

Figure 8. Should you pick stocks? Answer these three questions.

1.   Are you <u>interested</u> in picking stocks? My nieces are not. If you have no interest, why waste your time?
2.   Do you have <u>time</u> to pick stocks? Picking stocks is

not easy! You cannot make money by just picking up the newspaper and selecting a stock that looks good. There is a lot of work involved in finding the right stocks. And even hard work does not guarantee success.

3. Do you have the <u>knowledge</u> needed to pick stocks? If you are interested and have the time, but you know nothing about stocks, that will become a big problem. You can't just go into the stock market with no idea of what you are doing. Do you have 10 to 20 extra hours a week to devote to learning about picking stocks?

If you answered "yes" to all of these questions, then you may be up for the challenge of picking your own stocks.

However, in my experience, most people answer "no" to at least one, and usually all, of these questions. This means they should not buy individual stocks. Their best option is to reduce company-specific risk by owning a mutual fund.

What is a mutual fund? A stock mutual fund is a legal entity into which individuals add their money, so that a fund manager can invest that money across many different stocks. This allows one small shareholder to own a tiny slice of many stocks.

The majority of mutual funds in the world are actively managed, meaning that a fund manager actively attempts to pick stocks that she thinks will beat the market. Warren Buffett is one of the most well-known active fund managers. The objective of an active fund manager is to beat the market.

To do this, a fund manager may start by eliminating stocks that are at risk of crashing. A company and its stock might perform poorly because of the arrival of a new competitor, or because it has a high amount of debt, or just because it is badly managed. After eliminating these stocks, a fund manager will usually try to find and hold on to good stocks that are reasonably priced.

The main benefit you receive by investing with an active fund manager is that, because they buy many stocks, they immediately help you to reduce unnecessary company-specific risk. But there is one problem – it is hard to find an active fund manager who can consistently beat the market. In fact, it is very, very difficult to find that winning fund manager, before she becomes a winning fund manager, unless you happen to meet by chance. Furthermore, only a small number of people have the interest, time, and knowledge required to find such a fund manager. And even having these three things does not guarantee success.

Another thing to consider is that not all fund managers are working to help you. In the end, many are looking out for themselves. They will do their best for you, but the amount that they charge may be hurting you in the long run. So always bear in mind that it is up to you to take control of your financial situation.

In the world of finance, one surprising thing I often find is that the more you pay, the less you get. There are currently about 70,000 mutual funds available for you to invest in across the world, and about 80% of these are actively managed funds. Together, all those funds manage almost 25 trillion dollars.

The problem is that, as many academic studies[9] looking at the performance of fund managers have concluded, most actively managed funds *do not beat the market*. Why don't active fund managers outperform? They certainly get paid a lot of money to try to pick the right stocks!

Well, often that is the very reason they underperform. The return that you, the investor, receive is always after the fund manager's fees are deducted. If your fund manager is able to generate an annual 10% return, but his fees are 2%, then you, the investor, only receive an 8% return. The higher the fees, the harder it is for you to get a high return from an active fund manager. Besides fees, another reason that fund managers are unable to outperform is that the stock market is incredibly complex. Over and over again we have seen that no one can consistently predict the stock market.

Let's say you decide that, despite the costs, you will invest with an active fund manager. Research shows that your chance of finding the next consistently winning fund manager before they become "the next Warren Buffett" is tiny. The famous champion of shareholders' rights, John Bogle, wrote the seminal book, *The Little Book of Common Sense Investing*[10]. In it, he looked at 355 mutual funds that existed in 1970 and determined how many of them actually beat the stock market over the following 35 years. What he found was that only 24 funds managed to outperform over that time period. This means that an investor in 1970 had only a 7% chance that they would pick a mutual fund that outperformed over the long run. The point is that you picking the winner before she becomes the winner is not likely to happen. You should not begin investing unless you understand this.

Recently, I read an article about a young couple living in rural America in the 1960s[11]. They had $67,000 in savings for retirement and they didn't know what to do with it. The wife suggested that they give this money to a neighbor to manage, because she knew he had recently started managing other people's money.

In 1968, they asked that neighbor and he agreed to manage their $67,000. Twenty-seven years later, that initial $67,000 turned into more than $25 million, a massive 22% average annual return. Why? Because the neighbor to whom they gave their money was none other than Warren Buffett. But they did not find him through skill! It was just blind luck that led this couple to become incredibly rich. If Buffett had not lived near them, or if Buffett himself had not been lucky enough to pick the right stocks, the couple would probably never have earned such a fortune.

You must remember that if you invest in an actively managed fund, in order to outperform the market, as Buffett did for this couple, you will have to find a fund manager who will outperform *before* they actually outperform. This is incredibly hard to do.

Luckily, there is another option for the average investor who does not want to invest in an actively managed fund – it is called a "passively managed fund". The objective of a passively managed fund is to match the market's performance, not beat it. These funds do not make any bets on individual stocks or sectors, nor do they try to time the market, because they are not trying to outperform it. Most passive funds are also called index funds, meaning that they are trying to just match the stock market index. For consistency I will refer to these as passively managed index funds.

The benefit of passively managed funds is that they are low-cost, unlike actively managed funds. Their downside is that they are not "sexy". They are never going to beat the market, because they *are* the market. I believe that most people should invest their money in a passively managed index fund. If getting rich is your goal, you would be better served by focusing on building your wealth in business and investing in a passively managed index fund than you would if you were to cross your fingers and hope for your stocks or your active fund to succeed.

Now you know three ways you can invest in the stock market and take your finances into your own hands. You could own and manage your own portfolio of no less than 10 stocks (complicated and time consuming), you could own an actively managed fund run by a fund manager who you think is going to beat the market (hard to find, expensive, and probably won't outperform over the long run), or you could own a passively managed index fund that matches the market. For most people, the last choice is the right choice. This is the choice I recommend for you – keep reading to find out why.

Change the way you think about it:

- Most mutual funds are actively managed, meaning that they are constantly trying to beat the market.
- However, most actively managed funds *do not* beat the market.
- Your chance of finding a consistently winning active fund manager before they have their winning streak is very low.
- The alternative to an actively managed fund is a passively managed index fund, which buys all the stocks in a specific market and aims only to match that market, not beat it.

- For most people, investing in a passive fund is the right choice. This is the choice I recommend for you.

New terms:
- **Actively managed fund** – A fund in which the fund manager attempts to time the entry and exit into the stock market and into specific stocks. The main objective is to pick stocks that will outperform (or beat) the market.
- **Index fund** – A passively managed fund whose objective is just to match the stock market index.
- **Mutual fund** – Individuals pool their money into a fund, and a fund manager invests that money across many different stocks. It allows one small shareholder to own a tiny slice of many stocks. Each fund shareholder owns a proportional share of all the money in the fund.
- **Passively managed index fund** – A fund that makes no attempt to outperform the market, but rather tries to match the market. As a result, the fund is dramatically cheaper than an actively managed fund.
- **Sector** – Some companies that are in the stock market have similar businesses, for instance McDonalds and Burger King. We group similar stocks in sectors.

6. YOUTHFUL MISTAKES HURT MORE THAN YOU THINK

Have you ever heard someone say, "Make your mistakes while you're young"? Adults say this all the time! They think young people don't have much to lose, or that no matter how much money they do lose, they have time to earn it back. It may sound like good advice, but it can actually be disastrous for your financial future. My advice is to be especially careful to avoid financial mistakes while you are young. Errors made in your youth, even small ones, can be very painful later on. Here are three major mistakes related to investing to avoid at a young age.

Mistake #1 is to postpone investing. To understand the damage that can come from this mistake, let's consider an example (Figure 9). If you invest $12,000 per year ($1,000 per month) for 30 years, you will have contributed $360,000 by the end of the period. Assuming you earned an 8% return, through the magic of compounding, at year 30 you would end up with $1,468,000.

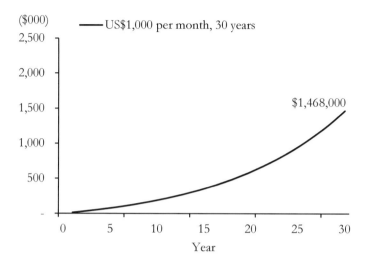

Figure 9. $12,000 invested per year for 30 years at 8% return.

Now let's suppose you make the mistake of postponing investing. Say you did not invest for the first 15 of those 30 years. Maybe you wanted to buy a car, or a house, or you thought your salary was too low, so you decided to wait until the second half of the 30-year period to invest your money. This would mean that if you wanted to invest the same $360,000, you would have to invest double every year – $24,000 per year instead of $12,000 – because you now have half the number of years to invest. Even though you put in the same $360,000 total, because it was only able to compound for you over the second 15 years, your final value would only be $704,000 (Figure 10). This demonstrates that the magic of compounding takes time to appear.

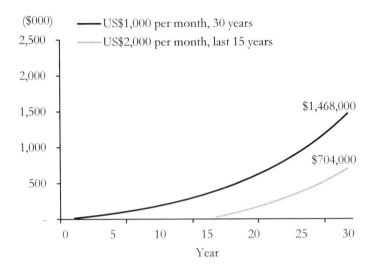

Figure 10. $24,000 invested per year in final 15 years at 8%.

Looking at the previous examples, what do you think would happen if you took that same $360,000 and invested it only in the first 15 years? Figure 11 shows that, amazingly, it would grow to become more than $2 million ($2,233,000 to be exact!). This is because this money would have had much more time to compound. From this we can see that equal money contributed in the first half of the period is worth more than three times the value of the money that was contributed in the final years.

Figure 11. $24,000 invested per year in initial 15 years at 8%.

Let's look at this example another way. Say that you determined that you needed $2,233,000 by the end of year 30. This example of contributing $24,000 per year for the first 15 years would get you there. And, it would mean only a total contribution of $360,000. But, if you invested equally every year, for each of the 30 years, you would have to invest $18,300 per year (for a total contribution over the years of $548,000). If you didn't start investing until the final 15 years, you would need to invest $76,100 per year to get there, which is a total of $1,142,000. This shows that when you postpone investing it just gets much harder to do in future periods.

Letting your money grow over a long period is the best thing you can do to ensure your financial success. You may enjoy spending your money in the moment, but if you do not start investing while you are young, you will pay for the mistake of procrastination as much as threefold.

Mistake #2 is losing money when you are young. Money

lost when you are young can never grow exponentially for you. Suppose, like in the prior example, you invested $12,000 per year ($1,000 per month) for 30 years. Assuming you earned an 8% return, at year 30 you would end up with $1,468,000.

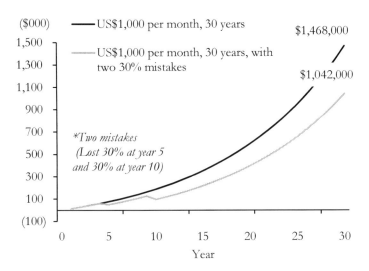

Figure 12. The damage caused by two youthful mistakes.

But what if you made a mistake? But let's say that five years into managing your money, someone tells you about an amazing stock that they think you should buy, you buy it, and it collapses. Boom! Your portfolio loses 30% in that year. Then, five years later, in the 10th year, some friends come up with the idea of starting a restaurant, you sell 30% of the stocks in your portfolio, and invest in what you think is a fantastic idea. Then, crash! The restaurant flops and you lose all that money, another 30% hit to your investment portfolio. From then on, let's assume you learned your lesson and you never make another big mistake for the rest of the 30-year period.

What happens to your money? The $1,468,000 you would have had at the end of year 30 now becomes $1,042,000, because you made your mistakes while you were young. You would lose 30% of your money due to two mistakes over 30 years. Due to the magic of compound interest, the impact of your losses is magnified, because every dollar lost is a dollar that is not compounding interest for you. If you follow the advice in this book, you should be able to avoid making mistakes while you are young. Of course, you should try not to make mistakes when you are older either!

Mistake #3 is overreliance on financial professionals. You do not want to make the mistake of listening to financial professionals too much. By now you know that financial professionals, whether knowingly or unknowingly, do not always work in your best interests, but studies, including my own, have shown that even when they want to help you, on average, they cannot beat the market.

When I was a financial analyst at an investment bank, like my peers, my goal was to make earnings forecasts, set target prices, and make buy, sell, or hold recommendations for individual stocks. Since that time, I have done my own research which has shown that no matter how hard-working or impressive a financial professional is, on average, they are rarely able to consistently beat the market; the best they can usually do is match it. In fact, when it comes to estimating what the price of a stock will be in a year, one of my studies showed[12] that 50% of the time, professional financial analysts in Asia were wrong by a margin greater than 30%! This is mainly because in the investment world, professionals are often paid to appeal to emotions by exaggerating their predictions. In my research I have found a pattern in their behavior: They are consistently overoptimistic in their forecasts at the beginning of each year, but by the end they become much less optimistic. Figure 13 shows this pattern happening over and over again.

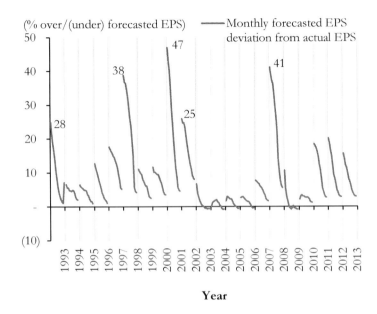

(% over/(under) forecasted EPS) ━━━Monthly forecasted EPS deviation from actual EPS

Year

Figure 13. Analysts start each year optimistic.

Further research I have done[13] shows that relying on analysts' forecasts cannot make us more money than just looking at the market ourselves and studying the past performance of any given company. And of course, this makes sense! If an analyst really had the secret to predicting the market, why would she share it? Why spread that knowledge around? She would have the chance to be the richest person alive! It would make no sense for her to sell that information. In conclusion, do not believe advisors or newsletters when they say they will sell you their secret. If they had one, they would not be selling it. Do not be tempted into believing that there is someone out there who knows.

Though it may seem that you have much less to lose when you are young, the reality is just the opposite. You must avoid the mistake of waiting to invest. Do not wait until you are older. Do not wait until the end of the year. Every day that you procrastinate is a day that the magic of compounding is not working for you. If you start investing early and avoid being overly dependent on financial professionals, you will be well on your way to a solid financial future.

Change the way you think about it:

- Making financial mistakes when you are young will damage your returns in the long run.
- Mistake #1 is postponing investing. Start investing as soon as you put this book down. The longer you wait, the longer the magic of compounding is not working for you.
- If you contribute equal amounts annually for 30 years, the first 15 are about three times more valuable than the second 15. This is due to the magic of compounding.
- Mistake #2 is losing money when you are young. Small errors when you are young will cause you to lose money, which will then no longer be able to compound for you over a lifetime.
- Mistake #3 is overreliance on financial professionals. No matter how smart they sound, or how much you want them to be right, most financial professionals do not beat the market. Remember – they cannot predict the future.

New terms:

- **Earnings forecasts** – Financial analysts, and most financial professionals, attempt to forecast the future profits that a company will make. They then use this forecast as a foundation for investment, shifting money into stocks of companies that they believe will beat the market in the upcoming year.
- **Recommendations** – The core function of a financial analyst is to assign a "Buy", "Sell", or "Hold" recommendation to a stock as a way of telling their clients which stocks to buy and which to avoid.
- **Target prices** – Financial analysts attempt to assign a price that they believe a particular stock will move to.

7. START BUILDING WEALTH THROUGH SAVINGS

In order to secure your financial future, you must save your money. It is not easy, but unless you are lucky enough to marry into wealth, you cannot build wealth without saving. Most people know that they should save, but do not realize just how much.

To start on this path, you must break the consumerist cycle that is so prevalent these days. We are all constantly bombarded with advertisements to buy things, but you will never build real wealth by buying everything you see. Instead, you should take pride in spending much less than you earn. One of the best books I ever read on this topic was *Your Money or Your Life*, by Joe Dominguez and Vicki Robin.[14] In it, the authors explain how to transform your relationship with money. One of the best things I learned from their book was to count and graph my monthly income and expenses. This exercise will help you understand the truth about what you are making and what you are spending. This is the starting point for investing, because without savings you cannot invest. I recommend you read the book and follow the authors' advice.

For many people, the trouble with living a frugal life is that nobody will see their wealth. They won't drive around in a fancy car or have expensive material possessions, and, of course, nobody will see their bank account and the money they are building up. But I challenge you to get your satisfaction from knowing that you can take care of yourself financially. The satisfaction of self-created, long-term security and independence far outweighs that of the short-term envy of those around you. This independence can be yours if you have the foresight to save and invest your money.

Some people are very good at being frugal and take satisfaction in cutting every cost as much as they possibly can. But also remember, that you cannot get rich by cutting costs alone. You can only cut so much out of your life. To move beyond cost-cutting and move toward building real wealth, you must find a way to increase your income over time. In my case, study and self-improvement allowed me to add more value at work, which led to higher income. While you find a way to achieve this, you should reduce any debt that you have, save to build up emergency cash, and then start setting aside money for investment every month.

Remember, it is up to you to make a financial plan that considers every part of your life. This book is meant to show you how to look at the stock market and help you understand the steps you can take to become financially independent; it is not designed to cover the specifics of every aspect of your personal and financial life. You must use the wisdom gained from this book and apply it to your own life.

To understand a bit more of the challenge of reaching financial independence let's consider a very simplified model of what it would take. In the following example, we assume that the person's only income in retirement comes from her portfolio; no pension, no social security, etc.

Meg is a 22-year-old college graduate. She was given a $20,000 graduation gift from her family, and is about to start her first job out of university. Let's assume she will earn the average starting salary for a college graduate in the US (as of 2014) – about $43,000 a year.[15] Let's also assume her salary will increase, so that halfway through her career it will be up 70% from her starting salary (figures based on the same survey). She wants to achieve financial independence at 60 years old, and thinks she will be happy at that point to live on the equivalent of her current monthly pre-tax income of $3,580. If she expects an 8% return from the stock market and a 4% return from bonds (we will discuss bonds later), then, to be financially independent at age 60, she would need to start investing $920 per month (about 26% of her monthly salary) today. Halfway through her career, the amount that she would need to invest would be equivalent to about 15% of her salary.

To build true wealth, you must focus on your financial independence and save, so that many years from now your investment income will pay for your expenses. However, you cannot reach that point unless you invest and leave your money in the stock market so that the magic of compounding can work for you. Do not spend your dividends and interest from your investments in any year – you must reinvest them. If you do not, you will be left with much less money than you would have earned through the magic of compounding.

Now that you understand the importance of saving your money throughout your life in order to build wealth, let's move on to Chapter eight.

Change the way you think about it:
- Start saving today. Right now. Take pride in how much you save, not how much you spend.
- Keep your monthly spending well below your income.
- Continue learning and growing so that you can add more value to the business that you are involved in, and can therefore earn more income from work.
- Follow these steps with your finances: First, reduce your debt; second, build up a cash reserve; third, invest every month.
- Focus on "financial independence"; this is when income from investments pays for your monthly expenses.

8. KEEP FINANCIAL COSTS AS LOW AS POSSIBLE

One of the most reliable predictors of successful investment performance is the degree to which an investor keeps their investment costs low. If you keep the costs you pay to financial professionals as low as possible, you will be more likely to earn a higher return on your money than even an active fund manager could. Unfortunately, most people never even consider the fees they are paying to financial professionals.

Imagine you want to buy a new TV. You walk into an electronics store and see an entire wall of TVs. The salesperson is there to help you, and explains why everything costs what it does. They might say that one is more expensive because it is a new model with higher resolution, or that the smaller ones are cheaper because they do not cost as much to make and deliver. By the time you leave the store, you understand what each TV costs and why. And of course, if you buy a TV, the salesperson will probably get a commission from your purchase. We view this commission as an acceptable source of their income.

The financial world is not much different, except that most individuals have no idea what fees or commission they are paying or how those fees are eating into their long-term wealth.

Remember this: Just like at the electronics store, nearly every person you come into contact with in the financial world is going to make their income from you. Of course, financial professionals cannot work for free, but you must always be careful not to pay too much. Always ask for a clear explanation of any and all fees you are charged. You can and should ask, "How does this option compare to that option, in terms of fees?" You, the customer, have the right to know what you are paying for, and it is your responsibility to ask. Any ethical financial professional knows that it is their duty to do their best to explain the fees you are paying when asked.

Let's consider some fees you pay when buying an actively managed mutual fund. According to the US Securities and Exchange Commission[16], there are two broad categories of expenses related to mutual funds:

Shareholder fees: You pay these fees when you buy, sell, or exchange mutual funds. They relate to the actual transaction of buying or selling.

Operating costs: These cover the costs of operating the mutual fund. Some of these expenses include: fees for managing the fund, marketing and distribution, legal, accounting, and other administrative expenses. These fees are taken each year from the amount of money you have invested in the fund.

If you had $100,000 at the end of one year, and the operating costs were 1%, then the fund management company would deduct $1,000 from your account that year. If your account grew to be $200,000 by the end of the next year then they would deduct $2,000 that year.

Shareholder fees

Name	Description
1 Sales load fee	Paid to brokers, by the fund management company- from your money, to cover their cost of selling the fund to you
2 Purchase fee	Paid to fund management company to cover costs of your purchase of the fund
3 Redemption fee	Paid to fund management company to cover the administrative costs when you sell a share in the fund you own
4 Exchange fee	Paid to fund management company if you exchange your fund for another within the fund management group
5 Account fee	Paid to fund management company to cover costs of maintaining the account, especially for small accounts

Annual fund operating fees

Name	Description
1 Management fee	Annually deducted from your money in the fund to cover cost of fund manager
2 Distribution fees	Annually deducted from your money in the fund to cover marketing and sales costs related to getting new investors
3 Other expenses	Annually deducted from your money in the fund to cover custodial, legal, accounting, and other administrative expenses

Figure 14. Detail of fees related to mutual funds.

The US National Association of Investment Companies[17] provides an excellent rundown on the mutual fund industry, completely free. It shows that the latest US active mutual fund's annual operating cost is about 1% of the amount you have in the fund vs. 0.14% for the average passively managed fund. This stark difference is due to the fact that:

1) Passively managed index funds only try to match the market. Therefore, there are no costs related to researching and selecting individual stocks. The only costs are administrative.

2) A passively managed index fund often focuses on investing in large companies, whereas an actively managed fund may look for smaller companies that might outperform. The search for these companies, as well as the cost of trading smaller stocks, raises the costs of actively managed funds.

3) Passively managed index funds are often much larger than actively managed funds, allowing the benefit of economies of scale.

Besides these explicit fees, depending on where you live and where you invest, taxes can become one of the largest fees of all. In some countries, there are taxes as high as 50% on your stock market gains. These are paid mainly when you sell your stocks. Because of this, if there ever comes a time when you want to sell a stock, it may not be in your best interest to do so – the tax rate might just be too high. You should focus on investing money in the stock market and leaving it there, because the less you sell and trade, the less you will pay in taxes.

Let's consider the impact of fees on your finances. If you are paying 1% of your assets to a fund manager each year, and you paid a sales charge of 1% when you bought the fund, that's 2% of your assets that you paid in the first year. This means that if the market had a 10% return in that year, the fund manager must outperform the market and earn a 12% return just to give you the stock market's return of 10%. As we have discussed in previous chapters, consistently outperforming the stock market is a very difficult thing to do. Having to make up for high fees makes it even harder.

The best way to reduce these excessive costs is to put your money in a passively managed index fund, rather than an actively managed fund. Different countries have different options for passive funds; the US is currently the leader in passive funds, and the funds are incredibly low-priced. Passive funds in other countries may be more expensive, but are usually still cheaper than active funds.

To better understand the cost difference between passive and active funds, let's assume that the long-term return of the stock market is 8% and that you have $1,000 to invest in a mutual fund now. You can invest it in an actively managed fund that charges a reasonable 1% management fee, or a passively managed fund, which charges a very attractive 0.20% fee. In 30 years, the $1,000 in the passively managed fund would grow to be about $9,500, while your $1,000 invested in the actively managed fund would grow to be only $7,600. This means you would end up with 20% less money at the end of the investment period than you would have if you had invested in the passive fund. In reality, 1% is a very low cost for an active fund. If you put your $1,000 in a higher cost 2% fee actively managed fund, your ending value would only be about $5,700, a massive 66% lower than if you put your money in a passively managed fund.

Putting your money in an actively managed fund that charges fees of 1% or even 2% would not be a problem if you could expect that active fund manager to outperform the market and make up for that fee. Unfortunately, you have already seen that this is an unrealistic expectation. You also now know that though there will always be a long-term outperformer such as Warren Buffett, your probability of finding him before he becomes successful is very low. Keep your financial costs as low as possible by investing in a passively managed index fund.

Now that you understand how to keep your costs low and the advantages and disadvantages of the different ways to invest, let's move on to Chapter nine.

Change the way you think about it:

- Make sure you understand what you are paying for, how much you are paying, and why.
- Actively managed funds can cost more than you think; passively managed index funds are almost always much cheaper.
- Successful long-term investment performance mainly comes from keeping costs low.
- Remember, nearly every person contacting you from the

financial world makes their income from your money.

- Depending on your situation, taxes could be one of your biggest costs. Taxes come when you receive income or gains, so try to minimize the realization of both when you are young, so that this money can compound for you.

New terms:

- **Operating costs** – These fees cover the cost of operating a mutual fund. Some of these expenses include: fees for managing the fund, marketing and distribution, legal, accounting, and other administrative expenses. These fees are taken each year from the amount of money you have in the fund.

- **Shareholder fees (Sometimes referred to as transaction costs)** – You pay these fees when you buy, sell, or exchange mutual funds. They relate to the actual transaction of buying or selling, so they are sometimes called transaction costs.

9. DIVERSIFY TO REDUCE RISK OF LOSS

If you are too conservative with your money, you expose yourself to "shortfall risk" – the risk that you will not have enough money at the end of your investment period. This can happen if you leave your money in the bank at a low rate of return, without investing it in the stock market. You can also create shortfall risk by making financial mistakes early on, like postponing investing or paying too much in fees. The best ways to reduce shortfall risk are to keep your allocation of money to the stock market high in your younger years, own a diverse portfolio, and keep your fees low.

In Chapter two we saw that company-specific risk is at its highest when you buy only one stock. If the riskiest thing to do in the stock market is to own one stock, then one of the least risky things to do is to own all stocks. To own all stocks is to diversify.

Today, it is easy and cheap to own every stock in the stock market. Various fund management companies offer passively managed index funds (or a similar instrument called an "exchange-traded fund" (ETF)), which own all the stocks in the stock market. Of course, when you own a portion of every stock in the stock market, you no longer get the excitement of picking that one stock that goes up by ten times. However, as we learned in Chapter five, even the professionals find that hard to do consistently, so what would be your chances? If you own all stocks in the market, your portfolio is diversified and can only be damaged by the entire stock market falling. But remember that over time the stock market always rises again, so that is not something to worry about – and, even if you only owned one stock, you would still be exposed to this risk.

The exchange traded fund is a relatively new instrument which acts almost identically to a mutual fund. One of the main differences is that because it trades as a share in the stock market, its low price makes it more accessible for a young person who is not able to invest a lot each time they invest. There are other small differences related to fees and trading costs, but these are small enough that they would probably not make much of a difference when compared to a passively managed index fund.

Below is a list of funds and ETFs that invest in the US stock market. To take one as an example, let's consider the Vanguard Total Stock Market ETF. Financial professionals often refer to a stock or ETF by its "ticker code" which in this case is "VTI". Every stock that you can trade in the stock market has a ticker code, in order to shorten the name. The ticker code can be directly related to the name of the company, but that isn't always the case.

From Vanguard's own website (Vanguard.com) we can understand a few things. The fee you pay to Vanguard to manage this ETF is only 0.05% of the total money you put in – one of the lowest management fees in the world! We can also see that the top stocks it currently holds in the ETF are Apple Inc., Exxon Mobil Corp., and Microsoft Corp. Since this is a passively managed index ETF, it is meant to match the US stock market, so it makes sense that such large-cap stocks would be a big part of the holdings. So, if you owned the VTI ETF, you could tell you friends, "Yes, I own Apple, Google, and Microsoft!"

Type	All US stocks	Code	Fee (%)	# of stocks
Fund	Vanguard Total Stock Market Index Fund	VTSMX	0.17	3,796
ETF	Vanguard Total Stock Market	VTI	0.05	3,796
Fund	Schwab Total Stock Market Index	SWTSX	0.09	2,504
ETF	Schwab U.S. Broad Market	SCHB	0.04	2,006
ETF	iShares Core S&P Total U.S. Stock Market	ITOT	0.07	1,503

Figure 15. Various stock funds and ETFs in the US.

To reduce risk further, you could also consider owning a passively managed international index fund or ETF, which would attempt to own every stock in the world. What's the benefit? Imagine that the U.S. stock market was going into a downslide, but that stocks in other parts of the world were going down less, or even going up. An international fund such as this would allow you to experience less of a downslide in your own portfolio, because the US would be only one of the countries you would be invested in.

Below (Figure 16) are a few funds and ETFs that invest across almost every stock market in the world. A look inside the iShares MSCI All Country World Index ETF shows the same stocks that were in the Vanguard VTI ETF, but also other large global companies such as Nestle SA and Novartis AG. This ETF holds stocks across more than 15 countries. About 50% of these are stocks of US-based companies, followed by Japanese companies, and then United Kingdom-based companies.

Type	All stocks in the world	Code	Fee (%)	# of stocks
Fund	Vanguard Total World Stock Index Fund	VTWSX	0.27	7,164
ETF	Vanguard Total World Stock	VT	0.17	7,164
EFT	iShares MSCI All Country World Index	ACWI	0.33	1,252

Figure 16. Various funds and ETFs of stocks in the world.

In summary, to keep company-specific risk as low as possible, I recommend you invest in a passively managed index ETF that owns stocks across the world. The only risk that will remain is the risk that the stock markets will fall, and as you now know, this is not something to worry about, because the stock market always bounces back over time.

Some people may be tempted to sell these ETFs when they think the stock market is too expensive and buy back when they think it is cheap. But you now know that the cost of doing that can damage your long-term returns. So, for your stock market investing, focus on buying one of the above ETFs and never buy any individual stocks or other funds again. You will get the benefit of owning stocks, without the risk of picking the wrong ones.

How much simpler could it get? For the rest of your life, just buy one ETF.

Change the way you think about it:
- Always try to reduce these four main investing risks:
- Company-specific risk – Reduce by owning a portfolio of stocks.
- Shortfall risk – Reduce by investing in the stock market and keeping costs low.
- Buying stocks at too high a price– Reduce by buying a little each month and not trying to time the market.
- Overexposure to one country or sector – Reduce by buying a fund or ETF that holds stocks in many countries and sectors.
- My best advice: buy a passively managed index ETF that owns all stocks in your country OR all stocks in the world.

New terms:
- **Shortfall risk –** The risk that you do not have the amount of money you planned on having at some future date. For instance if you wanted to have $5,000,000 at the age of 60, but you messed up and you only have $2,000,000, you

have a shortfall of $3,000,000.

- **Exchange-traded fund (ETF)** – An ETF is very similar to a mutual fund in that they both hold a collection of stocks, bonds, or other assets. The main difference is that you can buy and sell an ETF in the stock market just like a stock, unlike a mutual fund which must be bought from and sold to the fund-management company.
- **Ticker code** – The abbreviation which applies to the stock of each listed company. For instance, MSFT for Microsoft, GE for General Electric. ETFs also have ticker codes, since they trade like a stock on the stock market.

10. A MIX OF STOCKS AND BONDS IS VITAL

First, what is a bond? When a government or a company borrows money from a bank it is called a loan. When they borrow money from the public, they issue a bond. You give them money in exchange for a piece of paper, which is their word, or their "bond", that they will pay you back. What do you get in return? First, you get a regular interest payment (a "coupon" when referring to bonds). Next, when the bond expires, you give the borrower back the piece of paper and they return your money.

Because bonds involve fewer risks than stocks, their prices bounce around a lot less. In fact, at times their prices may even move in the opposite direction than the price of stocks. By holding bonds in your portfolio you benefit from both of these features. Think of it this way – suppose you had $200 to invest in your portfolio and you put $100 into stocks and $100 into bonds. Then assume that the bond portion went up to $110, but the stock portion moved in the opposite direction and went down to $90. Though you don't like the fall in the stock price, because it went down when your bonds went up, your portfolio value remained $200. In this way, bonds can reduce the amount that your overall portfolio bounces around over time. The bad news is, as you add bonds to your portfolio, because they pay you a lower rate of return, you reduce your long-term rate of return. However, you will soon see that the small reduction in return is more than offset by a large reduction in risk. The stability that bonds bring to a portfolio is vital to securing your financial future.

Figure 17 below shows the US stock market return each year over the past 112 years. I broke up the return into 10 ranges. For instance, the first range was between -40% and -30% return. The chart shows that in three years out of 112, the stock market fell by between 30% and 40%; the worst year was 1931 when it fell 39.8%. However, in one year, the stock market rose between 50% and 60%; that year was 1933, when the stock market rose 53%. This shows a very wide distribution of possible returns, but also shows that in most years the stock market gives a return of 0% to 30%.

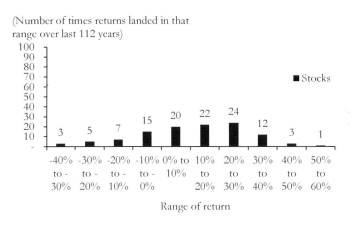

Figure 17. US stock market returns: the last 112 years.

Figure 18 shows the exact same chart, but with bonds added in. In 82 out of 112 years, bond returns were between zero and 10%. The most that bonds ever lost in one year over the past 112 years was 8% in 1994; in fact, there were only 13 cases of bonds having a negative return over this period. Compare this to the stock market which had 21 years of negative returns. And in 1982 the bond market gained 32.8%, its highest return over the period.

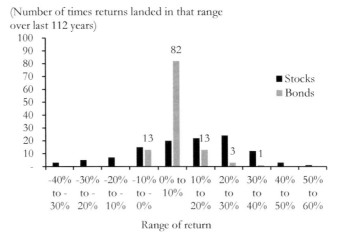

Figure 18. Returns for both US stocks and bonds.

From this we see that volatility is high for stocks and low for bonds.

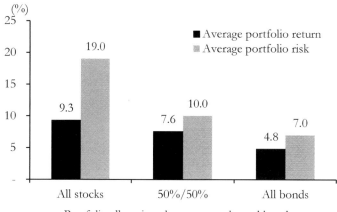

Portfolio allocations between stocks and bonds

Figure 19. Risk falls much faster than return when bonds are added.

The concept behind Figure 19 won Harry Markowitz the 1990 Nobel Prize in Economics. The figure shows that as you blend bonds into a stock portfolio, risk falls fast. In this case, I show the actual stock market and bond market returns over the past 112 years. If your portfolio owned all stocks, then your portfolio return would have been 9.3%, but if you decided to put only half of your money in stocks and the other half in bonds, your return would have been only 7.6%. This is about a 20% reduction in return. The good news is that the volatility of your portfolio would have decreased much more. Consider that if you owned only stocks, the volatility of the portfolio would be 19%. But, by holding half of your money in bonds, you would reduce the portfolio's volatility to 10%. This is a nearly 50% reduction in the volatility of your portfolio!

This shows that you can get a very large benefit in risk reduction versus your small reduction in return. Adding bonds to a portfolio reduces risk very quickly. If owning a diversified portfolio of 10 stocks or a passively or actively managed fund is like wearing a seatbelt in a car, adding bonds to your portfolio is like installing an airbag.

Bonds should be part of your long-term investment strategy, and now is the time to think about how you can blend them into your portfolio. As a general rule, in the first half of your life, you should own mainly stocks. In the second half, you should own mainly bonds. This ratio of stocks to bonds is something you should only adjust at certain, predetermined times, which you can write into your financial plan. All you really need to know is how much to invest in stocks versus bonds, and when to change the ratio.

To get to this ratio, the first thing to do is set a target of how much of your money should be in stocks at different times in your life. To do this, I recommend using this simple formula: 110 – your age = percentage of your invested money that should be in stocks. Then, every 10 years, you should adjust the percentage of stocks that you own. So, if you are 20 years old, 90% of your money should be in the stock market, with the other 10% in the bond market. This means that if you invest $1,000 per month, $900 should be invested in stocks while the remaining $100 should in bonds. Then, at age 30, you should target to have 80% of your money in stocks, and 20% in bonds. By the time you are 60 years old, you should own 50% stocks and 50% bonds.

Some finance books use the formula of 100 minus your age to get your target allocation in the stock market. However, I believe that if you have your seatbelt on (diversified stock portfolio) and your airbag installed (bonds included with your stock portfolio) it is okay to hold more stocks (110 minus your age, rather than 100) in your portfolio to maximize the power of compounding. Ultimately, there is no perfect formula, but the key is striking a balance between risk and return. Adding bonds to your portfolio reduces the volatility of your portfolio, but remember that if you add too many bonds, you increase your shortfall risk, which is very dangerous. This is why I use 110 minus your age, instead of 100: to strike a good balance between risk and return. If you own a diversified passively managed index fund, you reduce your company-specific risk to nearly zero, while maximizing your return.

In summary, stocks are the core of any long-term investment strategy. To reduce company-specific risk, you should own a large number of stocks. You cannot remove market risk, but this is not something to worry about because over the long run, the stock market always bounces back. Once you have your highly diversified stock portfolio, it's important to blend in bonds to reduce the volatility of that portfolio. However, you don't want to add too many bonds, or that will increase your shortfall risk.

YOUR SEATBELT: Reduce risk related to owning stocks

Types of Investment risks	What is the risk?	Owning fewer stocks	Owning more stocks
Company-Specific risk	One company's stock price falls	Increases	Decreases
Market risk	The whole market falls	No impact	No impact

YOUR AIRBAG: Reduce portfolio risk by owning bonds

Types of Investment risks	What is the risk?	Owning less equity	Owning more equity
Volatillity	Portfolio value swings widely	Increases	Decreases
Shortfall risk	Not enough money at retirement	Decreases	Increases

Figure 20. Wear your seatbelt and have an airbag installed.

As you get older and increase your allocation to bonds, you will see lower and lower returns in your portfolio. With both your seatbelt and airbag properly in place, you should now expect to earn about 6% return over your lifetime, not the 8%

to 10% mentioned in Chapter four (remember that that return was for stocks only). This return also does not consider fees and taxes. If you are very careful with your investing, you might be able to pay total fees and other costs over your lifetime that equate to only about 1-2% per year.

110 minus age	Percent of Portfolio in		Portfolio Return if Equity return=8% Bond return=4%
	Stocks	Bonds	
110 minus 20 =	90	10	7.6
110 minus 30 =	80	20	7.2
110 minus 40 =	70	30	6.8
110 minus 50 =	60	40	6.4
110 minus 60 =	50	50	6.0
110 minus 70 =	40	60	5.6
110 minus 80 =	30	70	5.2
110 minus 90 =	20	80	4.8
110 minus 100 =	10	90	4.4
Average			6.0

Figure 21. Expect about a 6% lifetime portfolio return.

This brings us back to the premise of this book. An overall 6% lifetime portfolio return, minus about 1-2% in fees and other costs each year, does not match up to the "sexy", exciting dream that many people have when they enter the stock market. However, once you have this portfolio in place, you will expose yourself to the best possible return you can get, balanced with the lowest possible risk. Having set these variables, you are left to deal with the main way you can make yourself rich in the stock market: contributing a lot of money early on and letting it grow for as long as possible.

Below, I highlight a short list of passively managed bond index ETFs which hold a blend of mainly government bonds in the US and (in some cases) outside the US.

Type	All bonds in the US	Code	Fee (%)	# of bonds
Fund	Vanguard Total Bond Market Index	VBMFX	0.20	7,477
ETF	Vanguard Total Bond Market	BND	0.07	7,477
ETF	iShares Core US Aggregate Bond	AGG	0.08	3,426
Type	Bonds outside the US	Code	Fee (%)	# of bonds
ETF	Vanguard Total International Bond	BNDX	0.20	2,985
ETF	SPDR® Barclays International Trs Bd	BWX	0.50	514
ETF	iShares International Treasury Bond	IGOV	0.35	551

Figure 22. Bond ETFs across the US and the world.

Remember, after setting your targeted mix between stocks and bonds according to your age, and allocating your funds to each, you must contribute regularly. You can set all the targets and make all the plans you want, but if you do not invest your savings regularly, all the financial knowledge you have gained from this book will be worthless.

I recommend contributing a portion of your income to your investments once a month. This is because waiting until the end of the year to invest your extra cash will give you time to be tempted to spend it, and investing could start to seem like a chore. If you contribute regularly, you will get in the habit of investing and help yourself become financially independent. Remember – take pride in how much you invest.

Change the way you think about it:
- Though it will lower your returns, blending bonds into your portfolio will dramatically reduce risk.
- In the first half of your life, own mainly stocks. In the second half, own mainly bonds.
- Adjust your allocation between stocks and bonds only at predetermined times, such as once every ten years. Determine these times in your written financial plan.
- For each decade of your life, the percentage of your

savings that should go toward buying stocks should be equivalent to 110 minus your age, (at 20 years old it should be 90%).

New terms:

- **Bond** – When you lend a government or business money, they issue you a document, or bond, that says they will pay you a certain interest rate every year, called a coupon rate. At the end of the term of the bond they will return your money and you return their paper.
- **Coupon** – When you put your money in the bank the bank pays an interest payment. A bond pays a similar interest payment, but with a bond it is called a coupon. In the very old days, bonds came as a big piece of heavy paper with a bunch of perforated cutouts that you ripped off and returned to the government or company to get your coupon payment. Another form of coupon clipping!
- **Risk/Volatility** – In the financial world, we often refer to volatility as risk. If you imagine two stocks moving from $10 to $100 over a year, one goes up in a direct line from $10 to $100, hence zero volatility. The other bounces up to $150 and then down to $5. The average investor would consider this stock riskier. But, an active investor who is trying to time the market and pick individual stocks may see it as an opportunity. For our purposes, to simplify, we consider volatility a risk.

11. DO NOT TRADE TOO MUCH

The stock market can get quite frenetic, and with the constant ups and downs, it's hard not to want to "play the market". People get so excited when their stocks go up that they watch the market like hawks and often get sucked into trading far more than they should. When investing in the stock market, patience is key. Trade as little as possible.

Actively trading in and out of stocks, funds, and ETFs brings two problems. First, there are costs involved every time you buy or sell (called shareholder or transaction costs). A broker or a fund manager somewhere has to do something to make your trade happen, and they don't work for free. Second, every time you trade, you run the risk of buying or selling at the wrong time, which can destroy the wealth you have built up. Do not convince yourself that you can get rich by trying to beat the market by actively trading stocks. It is a losing strategy.

You now know that you should start with the conservative expectation of an 8% return in the stock market. If you add in bonds, as you should, your long-term total portfolio return might go down to about 6%. Most investors then pay an active manager's fee of about 1%, so long-term return falls to 5%. Do not fool yourself into thinking that you can boost this return by trading in and out of the stock market. In the long run, this is unlikely. As we saw in previous chapters, building wealth in the stock market is not about high returns, it is about leaving your money in the market for a long time to get the benefit of compounding. It is also about contributing as much as possible, as soon as possible.

You can cause a lot of damage to your wealth by trying to time the market. Though most investors like to think that they are good at timing the stock market, over the long run they rarely succeed. Imagine that a passively managed index ETF that owned all stocks in the market went up on average by about 8% per year. Would the average investor actually earn that percentage? No. Why? Because the average investor has bad timing; they buy when the market is high and they sell when the market is low. Most investors believe that they will not make this mistake (overconfidence bias), but, in truth, most do.

One way to understand the damage bad timing can have on your investment performance is to calculate return in a way that takes into account the timing of when an investor puts money into a fund. The main thing to understand about the result of this calculation is that over the long run, bad timing is almost always damaging to your return. How damaging? Let's take a look.

One study on this subject estimated that the average investor loses over 1% of the market return each year due to their badly timed trading behavior.[18] Think about that for a moment. The average mutual fund investor's timing is so bad that they lose at least 1% of the total stock market return that they could have had, just because they wanted to try to time the market. If they had just bought and held their stocks, they would not have had this problem.

Let's review – why don't most people get rich in the stock market? First, the stock market return they should expect over the long run is about 8%. Then to reduce risk, they should blend bonds into their portfolio, doing this reduces that return to about 6%. Then they lose about 1% in fees to fund managers, and then I estimate about another 0.5% because of shareholder fees. In addition, they lose about 1% as a penalty for bad market timing. Finally, all the buying and selling will ring up a tax bill that I estimate at about 1%. It is hard to believe, but these costs are real. If an investor does not know what they are doing, they may think they are earning 8% per year in the stock market, but over the long run they may be earning much, much less than that.

Examples	Most people	You
Expected long term stock market return	8.0	8.0
Expected long term bond market return	4.0	4.0
Portfolio return: Blend of stocks and bonds	**6.0**	**6.0**
Fund manager fees	(1.0)	(0.2)
Shareholder & transaction fees	(1.0)	(0.1)
Portfolio return after fees	**4.0**	**5.7**
Penalty or cost of bad timing	(1.0)	(0.2)
Tax costs	(1.0)	(0.1)
Portfolio return after all fees and costs	**2.0**	**5.4**

Figure 23. The "You Won't Get Rich" return, versus most people's long-term return.

What you have learned so far is that by buying a passively managed index fund or ETF, you can reduce the fees you pay fund managers from 1% to about 0.2%. In addition, you can expect almost no shareholder fees, such as front end fees, because you are not using a financial advisor. Finally you can reduce the penalty you pay for bad timing and taxes by not trading in and out of stocks or funds at all. Of course, the situation will be different for each person, but my best estimates in Figure 23 show what potential return you can expect over the long term.

Be patient with the market, and do not stress out about what your portfolio is doing. If you leave your money alone, you will be much happier in the end, because you will reduce risk, lower your costs, and increase your returns! This will leave you with much more wealth than if you try to play the market.

Change the way you think about it:
- Reduce action. Invest your money and then let it be.
- In the financial world, action always leads to costs, and usually mistakes.
- The average investor may lose up to half their possible market returns, simply because of their own bad timing.

12. COOL HEADS WIN IN THE END

Remember, when you invest in the stock market, individual stocks might not always bounce back, but the market as a whole always does. Panicking usually makes things worse. In fact, I looked at the worst 29 months in the stock market since 1900 and asked the question, "By one year later, did the stock market recover?" What I found was that 67% of the time, the stock market had recovered by the time one year had elapsed. When I extended the period to three years, it was 80% of the time. Recovery within five years happened 86% of the time, and, amazingly, 100% of the cases recovered within 10 years.

Consider the research we saw in the last chapter, which showed that the average investor loses about 1% of their long term return due to poor market timing decisions. A "buy and hold" investor continues to contribute to their investment on a regular basis, and then just leaves their money alone. They do not sell their stocks or try to time the market.

We have probably all seen at least one active investor – the person who is always talking about how stock prices are doing, telling you about their stocks, and reading the business news reports. When we hear them talk, it seems so impressive! They sound like they are doing so well! Unfortunately for them, the truth is that trying to time the market and actively trading all the time will most likely harm them in the long run.

During a remarkable study of 66,000 individuals investing across America,[19] the stock market was up 18%. However, these investors as a whole earned only a 16.5% return, because of fees. Then the study got interesting! The researchers classified investors into two groups: the active investors and the passive "buy and hold" investors. They found that the active investors did not end up earning 16.5%, but rather 11%, reducing their earnings by almost 7% just from trading. Buy and hold investors ended up earning about 18.5%. This is why the researchers titled their paper "Trading is Hazardous to Your Wealth."

I did my own study to see what would happen if an investor was so panicky that they did not own stocks on the 10 days when the stock market went up the most (what I call the "10 best days") over a 10 year period. This happens more than you might think, because the best days usually come right after the worst days. If you constantly watch the market, panic on the worst days and sell your stocks, you will miss the best days that often come afterward. In this case, I looked at the US stock market over the last 10 years to see what would happen if someone missed the 10 best days. What I found was that if an investor started out with $100, instead of ending up with $177 at the end of the period, they only ended up with $127. So, in this case, by missing the 10 best days (out of the past 2,500 trading days), they lost 66% of their possible long-term gains.

There are many studies that show the harm you can do by trading too much. So why do people do it? Because it is fun?

In a 1979 study, Nobel Economic Prize winner Daniel Kahneman showed that for humans, losses hurt doubly bad; that is, humans feel the pain of loss 2.5 times more intensely than the pleasure of gain[20]. This means that if you lose 10% of your money, you feel about the same amount of emotion as you would if you gained 25%. This explains why we feel so strongly when we lose money. Unfortunately, if you succumb to this feeling of loss and panic and trade your stocks often, you could lose even more.

In "Your Money and Your Brain,"[21] by Jason Zweig , the

author shows that financial losses and gains create biological changes in your body, and that the neural activity of someone whose investments are going up happens *in the same area of the brain as the neural activity of someone using cocaine.* Not only that, but stock market loss is processed in the same part of the brain as mortal danger! When you are losing money, your brain triggers some of the same physiological changes as it would if you were about to be killed!

Zweig also found research that showed that if the average person sees a pattern two times in a row, they will naturally expect it a third time. Human minds look for patterns all the time, even where they do not exist. Stock market prices change randomly all the time, so do not let yourself be tricked into seeing patterns where they do not exist.

Finally, Zweig teaches us that anticipating financial gain is much more powerful than actually receiving it. You know the feeling – you work hard for months to accomplish something, you wake up early and work on it day after day, and you feel excited and happy that you are going to reach your goal! But then, when you finally do reach it, it can be quite anticlimactic, even disappointing. Our emotions affect our ability to make good financial decisions. If you let your emotions get the better of you, you are almost guaranteed to lose money in the stock market.

Let's play a game. Below are three graphs, each representing a stock that you need to either buy or sell. I want you to look at each one, and write whether you would buy or sell within 10 seconds of looking at the chart. Don't think about it too much, just quickly look at them and write down your answers.

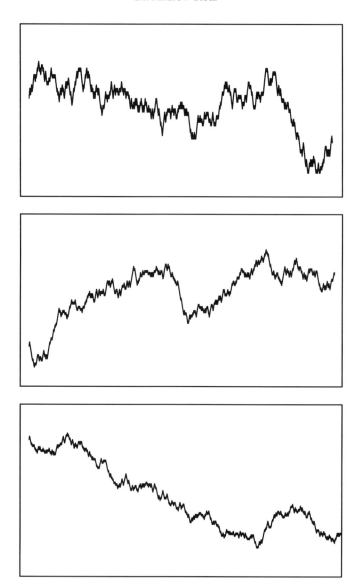

Figure 24. What do these three stock-price charts have in common?

Now that you have your guesses, the question is: did you notice what these three graphs have in common? Now look at them again. Can you spot it? Here it is: All three graphs were generated completely randomly. I made them up myself using the random number generator on my computer! You may have been pretty sure of your decision to buy or sell these stocks, but the truth is that your guesses were created completely based on your feeling about the graph. You were looking for patterns that weren't there.

The fact is, in anything governed by randomness, there will always be winners and losers, but there is no way to guarantee that you will be one or the other. So much of it is just a matter of chance.

Imagine a stadium filled with 100,000 people. Now let's say we ask them to stand up and flip a coin. Anyone who flips "tails" sits down. Probability theory shows that about 50,000 people would be left standing. If they all flipped a coin nine more times, there would be roughly 100 people left standing. These people would have flipped "heads" 10 times in a row. Did they do it through skill? Of course not! We know that flipping a coin is a fair 50/50 chance! They were just lucky!

In the stock market, it is easy to think that a person can get incredibly rich through their own skill, but normal statistics tell us that there are bound to be a small number of people who are particularly successful and a small number of very unsuccessful ones, with a lot of average outcomes in between.

Of course, you could ask, "What about Warren Buffett? I read his books, and I believe he achieved his financial success through skill." Well, remember that you are identifying him at the end of his career. There are a lot of books about how he did it; people are naturally going to want to explain his success. But, did you notice that no one wrote a book about the person who lost in the stock market 30 years in a row – the anti-Warren Buffett? That book would never sell! People may want to believe that Buffett achieved his success through skill, but based on probability, there is a real possibility that he could just be the lucky one.

73

Of course, there are times that skill comes into play in the stock market, and it would be hard to say that Buffett does not have it. From my years of experience observing active fund managers, I would say that there are three traits which make some of them successful: 1) They manage risk very well, trying to always avoid large losses, 2) They try to understand and take advantage of the behavioral biases of market participants, 3) The money they manage is locked into place so that investors cannot just remove it when the market was doing poorly. Of course, these skills must be learned over years of experience and even then the rules of probabilities still intervene, making some unsuccessful despite their excellent skills and hard work.

So, the next time you hear someone say that they made a lot of money because of their timing in the market, do not assume you can do the same. In all probability, if that person is not lying, they were just lucky. Following your emotions will lead you to financial failure. Instead, follow your financial plan and stick to it.

Change the way you think about it:
- Individual stocks do not always bounce back, but the market always does.
- If you panic and sell stocks you, will likely lose a lot of money in the long run.
- The average buy and hold investor can earn double what an active investor can.
- Stay cool and don't panic, because if you sell on the bad days you could miss the good days.
- Missing the 10 best days in the stock market over the last 10 years would have reduced your returns by 66%.

New terms:
- **"Buy and Hold" investor** – A term used to describe an investor who buys stocks and holds them for many, many years.

Congratulations!

You have now changed the way you think about the stock market. Below is a review of what you have learned.

1. Create a written plan and follow it
Be one of the few who has a financial plan, keep it simple.

2. Simplicity beats complexity; keep it simple
Wear your "seat belt" by owning at least 10 stocks.

3. Start early; time really is money!
Start now to benefit from decades of compound interest.

4. Be realistic about stock market returns
Running a business can make you rich, the stock market is for growing your wealth.

5. Do it yourself; pros don't always work for you
Remove the guesswork, buy a passively managed index fund or ETF.

6. Youthful mistakes hurt more than you think
Don't wait, start investing now, no one can do it for you.

7. Start building wealth through savings
Take pleasure in spending much less than you make.

8. Keep financial costs as low as possible
Keep fees and taxes low with a passively managed index fund.

9. Diversify to reduce risk of loss
Achieve diversification through a passively managed index fund that owns all stocks in your nation or the world.

10. A mix of stocks and bonds is vital
Own stocks in a ratio of 110 minus your age, the rest in bonds.

11. Do not trade too much
Reduce action. Invest, let it be, or risk big long-term losses.

12. Cool heads win in the end
In the long run, stock markets bounce back. Don't try to time the stock market, it's a loser's game.

Dr. Andrew Stotz

ABOUT THE AUTHOR

Dr. Andrew Stotz is an award-winning equity analyst with twenty years of experience working for various investment banks. He is the CEO of A. Stotz Investment Research, an independent research firm focused on stock selection and portfolio management in Asia. He has been a university lecturer in finance for all of those twenty years, and earned a PhD in finance from the University of Science and Technology of China. He is a co-founder of CoffeeWORKS Co. Ltd., a leading specialty coffee roaster, and Jcademy.com, an innovative online learning platform. Andrew has also authored the book, Transform your Business with Dr. Deming's 14 Points. He currently serves as the President of CFA Society Thailand and has been a Chartered Financial Analyst since 2001. He is an infectiously positive person, an avid yoga student, cyclist, and wellness aficionado.

BIBLIOGRAPHY

Barber, B. M., & Odean, T. (n.d.).

Barber, B. M., & Odean, T. (2000). Trading is Hazardous to Your Wealth: The Common Stock Investment Performance of Individual Investors. *The Journal of Finance, 55*(2), 773-806.

Bogle, J. (2007). *The Little Book of Common Sense Investing: The Only Way to Guarantee Your Fair Share of Stock Market Returns.* Hoboken, N.J.: John Wiley & Sons.

Buehler, R. G. (1994). Exploring the "planning fallacy": Why people underestimate their task completion times. *Journal of Personality and Social Psychology, 67*(3), 366-381.

Christensen-Szalanski, J. J. (1981). Physicians' use of probabilistic information in a real clinical setting. *Journal of Experimental Psychology: Human Perception and Performance, 7,* 928-935.

Clayson, D. E. (2005). Performance Overconfidence: Metacognitive Effects or Misplaced Student Expectations? *Journal of Marketing Education, 27*(2), 122-129.

College Board. (1976-1977). *Student descriptive questionnaire.* Princeton NJ , Educational Testing Service.

Dichev, I. D. (2004, December). *What Are Stock Investors' Actual Historical Returns? Evidence from Dollar-Weighted Returns.* Retrieved from Social Science Research Network: http://ssrn.com/abstract=544142

Dominguez, J., & Robin., V. (1999). *Your Money or Your Life, Your Money or Your Life: Transforming Your Relationship with Money and Achieving Financial Independence.* Penguin.

Fama, E. F., & French, K. R. (2010, October). Luck Versus Skill in the Cross-Section of Mutual Fund Returns. *The Journal of Finance, 65*(5), 1915-1947.

Goetzmann, W. N., & Kumar, A. (2008). Equity Portfolio Diversification. *Review of Finance, 12*(3), 433-463.

Henrion, M., & Fischhoff, B. (1986). Assessing Uncertainty in Physical Constants. *American Journal of Physics, 54*, 791-797.

Investment Company Institute. (2014). *Investment Company Fact Book; A Review of Trends and Activities in the U.S. Investment Company Industry, 54th Edition* . Retrieved from ICI Fact Book: http://www.icifactbook.org/fb_ch5.html

Kahneman, D., & Tversky, A. (1979, March). Prospect Theory: An Analysis of Decision under Risk. *Econometrica, 47*(2), 263-291.

Office of Investor Education and Advocacy . (2014). *Mutual Fund Fees and Expenses.* (O. o. Advocacy, Ed.) Retrieved from Investor Bulletin SEC Pub. No. 162 (5/14): http://www.sec.gov/oiea/investor-alerts-bulletins/ib_mutualfundfees.pdf

PayScale, Inc. (2015). *2013-2014 PayScale College Salary Report.*

Retrieved 2014, from Payscale.com:
http://www.payscale.com/college-salary-report-2014/full-list-of-schools

Presson, P. K. (1996). Illusion of control: A meta-analytic review . *Journal of Social Behavior & Personality, 11*(3), 493-510.

Princeton Survey Research Associates International. (2012). *2012 Household Financial Planning Survey.* Consumer Federation of America. Washington DC: Certified Financial Planner Board of Standards, Inc.

Shiller, R. (From 1989). *U.S. Stock Markets 1871-Present and CAPE Ratio.* Retrieved from Online Data Robert Shiller: http://www.econ.yale.edu/~shiller/data.htm

Stotz, A., & Lu, W. (2014, July 17). *Ten Stocks are Enough in Asia.* Retrieved 2014, from Social Science Research Network: http://papers.ssrn.com/sol3/papers.cfm?abstract_id=2461115

Svenson, O. (1981). Are we less risky and more skillful than our fellow drivers? *Acta Psychologica, 47*, 143-151.

Tsai, C. I. (2008). Effects of Amount of Information on Judgment Accuracy and Confidence. *Organizational Behavior and Human Decision Processes, 107*, 97-105.

Warner, B. (2014, May 4). *In 1965, A Man Asked His Neighbor To Manage His Modest $67,000 Savings. Guess Who That Neighbor Was....* Retrieved from Celebrity Net Worth: http://www.celebritynetworth.com/articles/entertainment-articles/1965-man-asked-neighbor-warren-buffett-invest-67k-life-savings-guess-turned

Westat. (2009). *National Consumer Survey on Personal Finance.* Washington: Certified Financial Planner Board of Standards Inc.

Williams, J. S. (2014). *DALBAR's 20th Annual Quantitative Analysis of Investor Behavior.* Retrieved from Grandwealth.com: http://grandwealth.com/files/DALBAR%20QAIB%20201 4.pdf

Zenger, T. R. (1992). Why do employers only reward extreme performance? Examining the relationships among performance, pay, and turnover. *Administrative Science Quarterly, 37*, 198-219.

Zweig, J. (September 2007). *Your Money and Your Brain: How the New Science of Neuroeconomics Can Help Make You Rich* (First ed.). Simon & Schuster.

ENDNOTES

Chapter 1. Create a written plan and follow it

[1] Overconfidence bias

Clayson, D. E. (2005). Performance Overconfidence: Metacognitive Effects or Misplaced Student Expectations? *Journal of Marketing Education, 27*(2), 122-129.

Christensen-Szalanski, J. J. (1981). Physicians' use of probablistic information in a real clinical setting. *Journal of Experimental Psychology: Human Perception and Performance, 7*, 928-935.

[2]

Westat. (2009). *National Consumer Survey on Personal Finance.* Washington: Certified Financial Planner Board of Standards Inc.

Princeton Survey Research Associates International. (2012). *2012 Household Financial Planning Survey.* Consumer Federation of America. Washington DC: Certified Financial Planner Board of Standards, Inc.

[3] Overestimation bias

Presson, P. K., and Benassi, V. A. (1996). Illusion of control: A meta-analytic review. *Journal of Social Behavior & Personality, 11*(3), 493-510.

Buehler, R., Griffin, D., and Ross, M. (1994). Exploring the "planning fallacy": Why people underestimate their task completion times. *Journal of Personality and Social Psychology, 67*(3), 366-381.

Zenger, T. R. (1992). Why do employers only reward extreme performance? Examining the relationships among performance, pay, and turnover. *Administrative Science Quarterly, 37*, 198-219.

College Board. (1976-1977). Student descriptive questionnaire. Princeton, NJ: Educational Testing Service. (In a survey of high school seniors, 25% rated themselves in the top 1% in their ability to get along with others)

Svenson, O. (1981). Are we less risky and more skillful than our fellow
    drivers? *Acta Psychologica, 47*, 143-151.

[4] **Expert overconfidence, physician overconfidence**

Christensen-Szalanski, J. J. (1981). Physicians' use of probablistic information
    in a real clinical setting. *Journal of Experimental Psychology: Human
    Perception and Performance, 7*, 928-935.

[5] **Physicists' overconfidence**

Henrion, M., & Fischhoff, B. (1986). Assessing Uncertainty in Physical
Constants. *American Journal of Physics, 54*, 791-797.

Chapter 2. Simplicity Beats Complexity; Keep it Simple

[6] University of Chicago students were asked to predict the outcome of
football games. Regardless of the amount of information provided,
participants were about 62% accurate. Confidence levels rose from 69% to
80% as the number of information points increased from 6 to 30.

Tsai, C. I. (2008). Effects of amount of information on judgment accuracy
    and confidence. *Organizational Behavior and Human Decision Processes,
    107*, 97-105.

Seductive details effect

Sanchez, C. A. and Wily, J. (2006). An examination of the seductive details
    effect in terms of working memory capacity. *Memory & Cognition,
    34*(2), 344-355.
    http://people.oregonstate.edu/~sancchri/pubs/seductive.pdf

Garner, R., Brown, R., Sanders, S., & Menke, D. (1992). Seductive details and
    learning from text. In K. A. Renninger, S. Hidi, & A. Krapp (Eds.),
    The role of interest in learning and development, 239-254. Hillsdale, N.J.:
    Lawrence Erlbaum.
    http://www.unco.edu/cebs/psychology/kevinpugh/motivation_p
    roject/resources/hidi_renninger_krapp04.pdf

Garner, R., Gillingham, M., & White, C. (1989). Effects of "seductive details"
    on macroprocessing and microprocessing in adults and children.
    Cognition and Instruction, 6, 41-57.

Harp, Shannon F.; Mayer, Richard E. (1997). The role of interest in learning
    from scientific text and illustrations: On the distinction between
    emotional interest and cognitive interest. *Journal of Educational
    Psychology, 89*(1), 92-102.

http://visuallearningresearch.wiki.educ.msu.edu/file/view/Harp+%26+Mayer+%281997%29.pdf

Harp, S. F., & Mayer, R.E. (1998). How seductive details do their damage: A theory of cognitive interest in science learning. *Journal of Educational Psychology, 90,* 414-434. http://visuallearningresearch.wiki.educ.msu.edu/file/view/Harp+%26+Mayer+(1998).pdf

Diversification

[7] Stotz, A., & Lu, W. (2014, July 17). *Ten Stocks are Enough in Asia.* Retrieved 2014, from Social Science Research Network: http://papers.ssrn.com/sol3/papers.cfm?abstract_id=2461115

[8] Goetzmann, W. N., & Kumar, A. (2008). Equity Portfolio Diversification. *Review of Finance, 12*(3), 433-463.

Chapter 3. Start Early; Time Really is Money!

Barber, B. M., & Odean, T. (2000). Trading is Hazardous to Your Wealth: The Common Stock Investment Performance of Individual Investors. *The Journal of Finance, 55*(2), 773-806. Available at SSRN: http://ssrn.com/abstract=219228 or http://dx.doi.org/10.2139/ssrn.219228

Chapter 4. Be Realistic About Stock Market Returns

[9] Fama, E. F., & French, K. R. (2010, October). Luck Versus Skill in the Cross-Section of Mutual Fund Returns. *The Journal of Finance, 65*(5), 1915-1947. Information originally accessed from the authors' December 14, 2009, Tuck School of Business Working Paper No. 2009-56 ; Chicago Booth School of Business Research Paper; Available at SSRN: http://ssrn.com/abstract=1356021)

[10] Bogle, J. (2007). *The Little Book of Common Sense Investing: The Only Way to Guarantee Your Fair Share of Stock Market Returns.* Hoboken, N.J.: John Wiley & Sons.

[11] Warner, B. (2014, May 4). *In 1965, A Man Asked His Neighbor To Manage His Modest $67,000 Savings. Guess Who that Neighbor Was.* Retrieved from Celebrity Net Worth: http://www.celebritynetworth.com/articles/entertainment-articles/1965-man-asked-neighbor-warren-buffett-invest-67k-life-savings-guess-turned

Chapter 6. Youthful Mistakes Hurt More Than You Think

[12] http://www.slideshare.net/andrewstotz/stop-wasting-time-start-adding-value-part-i-forecasting-34074988

[13] Idem, Endnote 12

Chapter 7. Start Building Wealth Through Savings

[14] Dominguez, J., & Robin., V. (1999). *Your Money or Your Life, Your Money or Your Life: Transforming Your Relationship with Money and Achieving Financial Independence*. Penguin.

[15] PayScale, Inc. (2015). *2013-2014 PayScale College Salary Report*. Retrieved 2014, from Payscale.com: http://www.payscale.com/college-salary-report-2014/full-list-of-schools

[16] U.S. Securities and Exchange Commission. (2014). *Mutual Fund Fees and Expenses*. (O. o. Advocacy, Ed.) Investor Bulletin SEC Pub. No. 162 (5/14). Retrieved from: http://www.sec.gov/oiea/investor-alerts-bulletins/ib_mutualfundfees.pdf

[17] Investment Company Institute (2014). *Investment Company Fact Book; A Review of Trends and Activities in the U.S. Investment Company Industry, 54th Edition* . Retrieved from ICI Fact Book: http://www.icifactbook.org/fb_ch5.html

Chapter 11. Don't Trade Too Much

[18] Dichev, I. D. (2004, December). *What are Stock Investors Actual Historical Returns? Evidence from Dollar-Weighted Returns*. Retrieved from Social Science Research Network: http://ssrn.com/abstract=544142

Chapter 12. Cool Heads Win in the End

[19] Barber, B. M., & Odean, T. (2000). *Trading is Hazardous to Your Wealth: Common Stock Investment Performance of Individual Investors. The Journal of Finance, 55(2), 773-806*. Available at SSRN: http://ssrn.com/abstract=219228

[20] Kahneman, D., & Tversky, A. (1979, March). Prospect Theory: An Analysis of Decision under Risk. *Econometrica, 47*(2), 263-291. Available here: http://www.princeton.edu/~kahneman/docs/Publications/prospect_theory.pdf

[21] Zweig, J. (September 2007). *Your Money and Your Brain: How the New Science of Neuroeconomics Can Help Make You Rich* (First ed.). Simon & Schuster.

41930470R00057